WOMEN WHO WIN

Cynthia Cooper

Mia Hamm

Martina Hingis

Chamique Holdsclaw

Michelle Kwan

Lisa Leslie

Sheryl Swoopes

Venus & Serena Williams

CHELSEA HOUSE PUBLISHERS

WOMEN WHO WIN

LISA LESLIE

Brent Kelley

Introduction by
HANNAH STORM

CHELSEA HOUSE PUBLISHERS
Philadelphia

Frontis: *Superstar of the Los Angeles Sparks, Lisa Leslie's athletic prowess and record-breaking play has earned her the nickname "Queen of the Boards."*

Produced by
21st Century Publishing and Communications, Inc.
New York, New York
http://www.21cpc.com

CHELSEA HOUSE PUBLISHERS

Editor in Chief: Stephen Reginald
Managing Editor: James D. Gallagher
Production Manager: Pamela Loos
Art Director: Sara Davis
Director of Photography: Judy L. Hasday
Senior Production Editor: J. Christopher Higgins
Publishing Coordinator: James McAvoy
Project Editor: Anne Hill

The Chelsea House World Wide Web address is
http://www.chelseahouse.com

First Printing

1 3 5 7 9 8 6 4 2

Library of Congress Cataloging-in-Publication Data

Kelly, Brent P.
   Lisa Leslie / Brent Kelly; introduction by Hannah Storm.
   p. cm. – (Women who win)
   Includes bibliographical references and index.
   Summary: Presents a biography of the star player for the Los Angeles Sparks of the Women's National Basketball Association.
   ISBN 0-7910-5794-1 (hc) — ISBN 0-7910-6154-X (pb)
   1. Leslie, Lisa, 1972– —Juvenile literature. 2. Basketball players—United States—Biography—Juvenile literature. 3. Women basketball players—United States—Biography—Juvenile literature. [1. Leslie, Lisa, 1972– . 2. Basketball players. 3. Women—Biography. 4. Afro-Americans—Biography.] I. Title. II. Series.
   GV884.L47 K45 2001
   796.323'092—dc21
   [B]   00—027963
                                                                              CIP
                                                                               AC

Contents

INTRODUCTION   6

CHAPTER 1
THE FIRST ALL-STAR MVP   9

CHAPTER 2
"WHY DON'T YOU PLAY BASKETBALL?"   15

CHAPTER 3
ALL-AMERICAN   21

CHAPTER 4
OLYMPIC GLORY   27

CHAPTER 5
A PROFESSIONAL LEAGUE FOR WOMEN   33

CHAPTER 6
AGAINST THE ODDS   41

CHAPTER 7
GOING FOR ALL THE MARBLES   49

CHAPTER 8
IN THE REAL WORLD   55

STATISTICS   61
CHRONOLOGY   62
FURTHER READING   62
INDEX   64

WOMEN WHO WIN

Hannah Storm
NBC Studio Host

You go girl! Women's sports are the hottest thing going right now, with the 1900s ending in a big way. When the U.S. team won the 1999 Women's World Cup, it captured the imagination of all sports fans and served as a great inspiration for young girls everywhere to follow their dreams.

That was just the exclamation point on an explosive decade for women's sports—capped off by the Olympic gold medals for the U.S. women in hockey, softball, and basketball. All the excitement created by the U.S. national basketball team helped to launch the Women's National Basketball Association (WNBA), which began play in 1997. The fans embraced the concept, and for the first time, a successful and stable women's professional basketball league was formed.

I was the first ever play-by-play announcer for the WNBA—a big personal challenge. Broadcasting, just like sports, had some areas with limited opportunities for women. There have traditionally not been many play-by-play opportunities for women in sports television, so I had no experience. To tell you the truth, the challenge I faced was a little scary! Sometimes we are all afraid that we might not be up to a certain task. It is not easy to take risks, but unless we push ourselves we will stagnate and not grow.

Here's what happened to me. I had always wanted to do play-by-play earlier in my career, but I had never gotten the opportunity. Not that I was unhappy— I had been given studio hosting assignments that were unprecedented for a woman and my reputation was well established in the business. I was comfortable in my role . . . plus I had just had my first baby. The last thing I needed to do was suddenly tackle a new skill on national television and risk being criticized (not to mention, very stressed out!). Although I had always wanted to do play-by-play, I turned down the assignment twice, before reluctantly agreeing to give it a try. During my hosting stint of the NBA finals that year, I traveled back and forth to WNBA preseason games to practice play-by-play. I was on 11 flights in 14 days to seven different cities! My head was spinning and it was no surprise that I got sick. On the day of the first broadcast, I had to have shots just so I could go on the air without throwing up. I felt terrible and nervous, but

I survived my first game. I wasn't very good but gradually, week by week, I got better. By the end of the season, the TV reviews of my work were much better—*USA Today* called me "most improved."

During that 1997 season, I witnessed a lot of exciting basketball moments, from the first historic game to the first championship, won by the Houston Comets. The challenge of doing play-by-play was really exciting and I loved interviewing the women athletes and seeing the fans' enthusiasm. Over one million fans came to the games; my favorite sight was seeing young boys wearing the jerseys of female players—pretty cool. And to think I almost missed out on all of that. It reinforced the importance of taking chances and not being afraid of challenges or criticism. When we have an opportunity to follow our dreams, we need to go for it!

Thankfully, there are now more opportunities than ever for women in sports (and other areas, like broadcasting). We thank women, like those in this series, who have persevered despite lack of opportunities—women who have refused to see their limitations. Remember, women's sports has been around a long time. Way back in 396 B.C. Kyniska, a Spartan princess, won an Olympic chariot race. Of course, women weren't allowed to compete, so she was not allowed to collect her prize in person. At the 1996 Olympic games in Atlanta, Georgia, over 35,600 women competed, almost a third more than in the previous Summer Games. More than 20 new women's events have been added for the Sydney, Australia, Olympics in 2000. Women's collegiate sports continues to grow, spurred by the 1972 landmark legislation Title IX, which states that "no person in the United States shall, on the basis of sex, be excluded from participation in, be denied the benefits of, or be subjected to discrimination under any educational program or activity receiving federal financial assistance." This has set the stage for many more scholarships and opportunities for women, and now we have professional leagues as well. No longer do the most talented basketball players in the country have to go to Europe or Asia to earn a living.

The women in this series did not have as many opportunities as you have today. But they were persistent through all obstacles, both on the court and off. I can tell you that Cynthia Cooper is the strongest woman I know. What is it that makes Cynthia and the rest of the women included in this series so special? They are not afraid to share their struggles and their stories with us. Their willingness to show us their emotions, open their hearts, bare their souls, and let us into their lives is what, in my mind, separates them from their male counterparts. So accept this gift of their remarkable stories and be inspired. Because *you*, too, have what it takes to follow your dreams.

1

THE FIRST
ALL-STAR MVP

Being the first to achieve an honor is an experience that no one can take away, even though others may earn that honor later. In 1999, Lisa Leslie, the outstanding center of the Los Angeles Sparks, was named Most Valuable Player (MVP) of the very first All-Star game of the Women's National Basketball Association (WNBA).

It was not the first honor or award that Lisa had ever won. She was a three-time All-American in college, National Player of the Year, National Freshman of the Year, Naismith College Player of the Year, All-WNBA selection, and a member of numerous all-star teams. These had all been on-going honors, however, and Lisa was just a name on some lists. Several impressive players were included on these lists, but Lisa will forever be the first MVP of the 1999 WNBA All-Star game.

The WNBA began its inaugural season in 1997, and in its first two years was playing to establish itself in the highly competitive world of professional sports. The competition for fans included baseball, football, men's

---

Holding her Most Valuable Player trophy, Lisa speaks to an interviewer after winning the award for her outstanding play in the 1999 WNBA All-Star game. Lisa is no stranger to awards, but being named MVP of the first All-Star game was a special honor, which she felt made her part of the history of women's basketball.

basketball, hockey, tennis, and the American Basketball League (ABL)—another women's professional league. By the beginning of the 1999 season, however, the ABL had folded, and the WNBA took over. The league developed strong franchises, encouraged rivalries between regional teams, and attracted a devoted following of fans from all over the country. Further expansion was planned for 2000, when four new teams would be added to the league. The future was bright indeed.

All-star games have tremendous fan appeal because, in most sports, the fans get to choose the starting lineups by voting. The games also showcase the very best performers that a particular sport has to offer and draw television viewers who might otherwise never see a game. For these reasons, the potential to build new fans is excellent. The WNBA recognized all of this and knew the time had come for the first WNBA All-Star game to be played.

New York City's famous Madison Square Garden was chosen as the site, and July 14, 1999, was the date. All that was left was to select the players.

The game was to pit the best players from the Eastern Conference against the best players from the Western Conference, and the starters were to be decided by votes from the fans. The voting for the Eastern Conference starters was close and hotly contested at most positions.

For the Western Conference, the voters had clear choices for four of the five starters. Three players of the defending league-champions, the Houston Comets, were overwhelmingly chosen to start, including the top overall vote-getter, forward Sheryl Swoopes. Lisa Leslie, who received 66,219 votes, was the easy winner

for starting center, receiving nearly 20,000 more votes than runner-up Jennifer Gillom of the Phoenix Mercury.

There was no question that Lisa's selection was well deserved. At the time of the game, she was the Sparks' leader in nearly everything: scoring, rebounding, three-pointers (a very rare ranking for a center), and blocked shots. She was also in the top five or better in the Western Conference in most of these categories. It's hard to imagine that anyone did *not* vote for her.

Scores of young people surround Lisa as she signs autographs. As one of the most popular stars of the WNBA, Lisa is a role model for young women, encouraging them to enter the world of sports and showing that, like her, they too can be basketball heroes.

There was a problem, however. As the All-Star game drew near, Lisa was not playing as well as she usually did. She had recently suffered a mild wrist injury in a fall on the court and, although the injury was not serious, she was unable to handle the ball with her normally deft touch.

Neither she nor her team publicized the injury. When Western Conference All-Star coach Van Chancellor of the Houston Comets was asked at a pregame press conference how he thought Lisa's wrist injury would affect her play and how he would handle her, he replied that he didn't even know she had a wrist injury. He added that the best way to handle Lisa is just to let her play.

July 14, the day of the game, arrived. In the pregame warm-ups, Lisa's wrist did not appear to be giving her problems, as she demonstrated by her moves and shots before the sellout crowd of more than 18,000 at Madison Square Garden. She even dunked one shot. Her wrist did hurt, though, especially on the dunk. Lisa was not going to let it stop her from playing, however.

Lisa is 6' 5" tall, and two other Western Conference All-Stars were 6' 3". Only one Eastern Conference All-Star was that tall. When the game began, the West's height and strength advantages were too much for the shorter East squad to overcome. The West, led by Lisa's early drives, jumped to a 10-0 lead before the East could score and then pulled out to a 17-2 lead. At halftime, the score was 43-29 as Lisa, Sheryl Swoopes, and Cynthia Cooper combined for 21 points. The final score was West 79, East 61. Lisa's 13 points in only 17 minutes of playing time were the second most scored in the game.

Immediately after the game, Lisa was asked if it was hard for her to focus on the game with all the activities and distractions going on around her. An all-day street festival was organized for the fans and players, and there were numerous interviews and endless autograph requests. She answered, "Once we started from jump ball we're focusing, hoping you make all your shots. I felt very relaxed."

After learning she had been named Most Valuable Player, Lisa commented, "I felt really honored to have this award. Obviously, a few other players probably had the opportunity to get it as well." She was quick to give credit to others, adding, "I just thank God for blessing me to be here, to play. . . . I was able to get in and get some quick shots with Michele Timms pushing the ball up court. I thought the crowd was great. They got me totally fired up and the atmosphere was awesome! Phenomenal!"

Lisa was well aware of the significance of being named MVP, saying, "I guess basically I'll leave here believing that I'm going to be a part of history, being the first MVP." Later, she was asked, "Who do you think is the best player in the WNBA right now?" Without blinking, she answered, "As of today, ME!" And then, she laughed heartily.

2

"WHY DON'T YOU PLAY BASKETBALL?"

Basketball was not always part of Lisa Leslie's plans. In fact, at one point when growing up, she actually hated the idea of playing the game.

Lisa was born on July 7, 1972, in Inglewood, California, and, for her first four years, life seemed normal. When her father left the family, however, little Lisa's life changed. He left her mother, Christine, and her two sisters, Dionne and Tiffany, on their own. Over the years Lisa only saw her father once, and when she was 12, he died. Although Lisa's father occasionally sent the family a little money, he had not been supportive of his daughters as they grew up.

Life was tough for the Leslie family, but Lisa's mom was tough too. To support her three children, Christine became a truck driver, purchasing her own 18-wheeler. Later she remarried and four half-brothers were added to the family. Through the years and still today, Christine is the woman Lisa most admires.

Before Christine remarried, however, driving a truck kept her on the road and away from home most of the time. The girls lived with their aunt when Christine was

---

Lisa shares a ball with a little fan. As a child, Lisa was embarrassed by her height and brushed aside those who kept asking why she didn't play basketball. It wasn't until her teens that she realized her potential as a great player and began her rise to success on the court.

away and, although their aunt took good care of them and saw to all their needs, they missed their mother terribly. Lisa and her sisters eagerly anticipated the time when school was out for the summer and they could ride with their mom, hauling cargo all over the country. To save money, which was a constant problem for the family, Christine and the girls slept in a small sleeping area behind the truck's cab. Still, it was worth the discomfort to be together as a family.

Although she hated being away from her mother for the many long periods when school was in session, Lisa adjusted, matured, and grew. Her height was no accident. Christine herself was 6' 3". By the seventh grade, Lisa was 6'. People commented about her height, and classmates teased her. "Why don't you play basketball?" everyone kept asking.

Rather than seeing her stature as a potential asset, Lisa was embarrassed by it. Because of the incessant questions about basketball, she developed a dislike for the game, telling people that she hated it. Instead of glory on the court, Lisa's goal in life was to be a weather reporter, a goal she dreamed of from the time she was seven years old.

Becoming a weather reporter would be years away, however. In the meantime, basketball beckoned. When a friend, Sharon Hargrove, who also went on to play college basketball, convinced Lisa to go out for the junior high school team, Lisa found, to her surprise, that she liked playing. "I just changed my whole attitude," she explained. "I guess it was my destiny but I never knew it."

Although being tall is a great advantage for a basketball player, the game is difficult to master, and playing well requires much more than physical size. Lisa's older cousin, Craig, saw how she enjoyed playing and decided to help her. He recognized her potential, as well as her weaknesses, and he drove her hard to improve on what nature had given her. Whenever the time allowed, Craig made Lisa work out. She did push-ups and sit-ups, performed basketball drills, and shot baskets by herself. When the neighborhood boys were on the playground, Craig had Lisa were there too, playing with and against them.

Craig's efforts and Lisa's perseverance paid off handsomely. As a 6' 3" freshman at Morningside High School in Inglewood, she not only made the varsity team but started every game. The young athlete also excelled in other areas. She played high school volleyball, was a champion high jumper, maintained a near-A average in her grades, and was class president three years in a row.

In the summer between her junior and senior years, Lisa played on the Junior World Championship team, and college scouts who had not seen her before were now totally aware of her skills. The best was yet to come, however. By the time Lisa's senior year began in 1989, she was the most heavily recruited high school basketball player in the country. Every college wanted her. Only 17 years old and 6' 5", she was far and away the best high school player in the United States.

Lisa's senior year was one to remember. Her coach at Morningside High, Frank Scott, frequently had to take her out of games at halftime to allow her teammates to get in some playing time. Nonetheless, she averaged more than 27 points and 15 rebounds a game and skillfully

Lisa smiles and flips the ball after Morningside High's game with South Torrance. A teenage powerhouse, Lisa showed what she could do when she scored 101 points in the first half of the game, setting a new school record.

blocked the shots of anyone daring enough to try to put one up near her.

Lisa's final high school game was perhaps the most amazing single performance in basketball history. Morningside was playing South Torrance High School, and Coach Scott directed his players to get the ball to Lisa so she could try to break Morningside's single-game scoring record.

Her teammates came through, getting the ball to Lisa so that she scored a phenomenal 49 points in the first quarter. Then she came back with 52 in the second, giving her 101 at half-time, at which point Morningside led 102-24. Not only did Lisa set a new school record, she was only five points away from breaking the all-time single-game high school record, set seven years earlier by Cheryl Miller.

Coach Scott planned to let Lisa start the second half, score those five points, and then take her out. It was not to be. The South Torrance team, already reduced by two players who fouled out and one who was injured, was thoroughly embarrassed and refused to play the second half. The game was ruled a forfeit. "That was probably the highlight of my career," Lisa still claims.

As a result of her outstanding play throughout the season, Lisa was named the Naismith Prep Player of the Year. One of the most prestigious awards in the sports world, the Naismith is named for James Naismith, who founded basketball in the late 1890s. The award is given annually to the best amateur male and female basketball players at both the high school and college level. Further honors came her way when she was All-State and a unanimous high school All-American as well as the Gatorade and *USA Today* Prep Player of the Year. As the number-one high school prospect in the nation, and a recruiter's dream player, Lisa was ready to choose her college.

3

ALL-AMERICAN

Most of the coaches and scouts who had been after Lisa made many promises and appealing offers. A typical 17-year-old would have found such attention overwhelmingly confusing and probably would have found it difficult to make a choice. For Lisa, however, the decision was easy.

More than anything, she wanted her mother to watch her play, so she accepted the scholarship offered by the University of Southern California (USC), which was a natural choice. The best high school player ever to come out of that area would be going to her hometown college. It was a perfect fit.

In her very first game as a college freshman, on November 11, 1990, Lisa led the Lady Trojans of USC to an 88-77 victory over a tough and determined University of Texas squad. She scored 30 points, took 20 rebounds, blocked two shots, and had four steals. Nine days later, she pulled down 23 rebounds against San Diego State. Lisa's early performances provided college basketball fans a glimpse of what was to come.

Lisa's high school record brought her numerous offers for college scholarships. Choosing the University of Southern California, the young star earned All-American honors three times and was the National Women's Player of the Year in 1994.

Lisa ended her first year in college as the leading freshman scorer, averaging 19.4 points per game. She also finished as the leading rebounder, pulling down an average of 10 per game, surpassing everyone else in the country. The first freshman ever to be named to the Women's College Basketball Pacific Ten's All-PAC-10 team, Lisa was also chosen as the National and PAC-10 Freshman of the Year. A further achievement unheard of for a college freshman was being named the PAC-10 Player of the Week three times. Then, to top it all off, USC went to the National Collegiate Athletic Association (NCAA) tournament.

The summer following Lisa's outstanding college debut, she joined the gold-medal-winning team at the World University Games. When she slam-dunked before the game versus Spain, she got the rapt attention of the crowd. Dunking by women was not a play fans were accustomed to seeing, and all eyes were riveted on Lisa.

Lisa says she has been able to dunk since she was a freshman in high school and that she learned the move from her high jumping on the high school track team. She doesn't dunk in games now for fear of an injury to herself or an opponent. "I have done most of my dunking at high school pep rallies or pre-game warmups," she explained.

Lisa's sophomore year was even better. Hard work improved her defensive skills, and with hours and hours of practice, her offensive moves were even more awesome. She raised her scoring average to 20.4 points per game and her rebound average to 8.4.

Again, she was named All-PAC-10 as well as being posted to the All-American team. Lisa was further honored as the only sophomore nominated for the Naismith College Player of the Year Award. Lisa once again led USC's Lady Trojans at the NCAA tournament and concluded her sophomore year playing with the gold-medal-winning Jones Cup team.

Lisa's junior year again found her high atop the honors lists. She was All-PAC-10, All-American, and a finalist for the Naismith. Her games averaged 18.7 points and 9.8 rebounds, and for the third time, she led USC into the NCAA tournament. That summer, she played for the World Championship qualifying team and was named the USA Basketball Player of the Year.

As exceptional as Lisa had been her first three years in college, she was even more out-standing as a senior. As well as being acclaimed the National Player of the Year, she and the rest of the USC team played in the NCAA tourna-ment for the fourth time, where the team went all the way to the quarterfinals. The first player in PAC-10 history to be named All-PAC-10 four times, Lisa was also an All-American for the third time. She earned a Kodak All-American Award and won the Naismith Award, just as she had done as a high school senior. Nearly all observers and fans agreed that Lisa Leslie was one of the finest basketball players in the country.

When Lisa's college career was over and all the counting was completed, she held PAC-10 records for total points (2,414), rebounds (1,214), and blocked shots (321). In four years of college play at the highest level, she had averaged 20.1 points, 10.1 rebounds, and 2.7 blocked shots per game. She made an unbeliev-able 53.4 percent of her shot attempts from the field and averaged nearly two steals a game

Playing in Italy gave Lisa added experience, while she continued her impressive performances on the court. Although she enjoyed Italy's old-world cities and culture as well as its exuberant fans, she stayed only one season, returning home to try out for one of her special goals—to play in the Olympics.

(228 in four years), a huge number for a center.

Lisa was possibly one of the best female basketball players in history at that point, and certainly one of the best in the country. However, upon graduation from USC, she had no place to play. No professional women's teams or leagues existed in the United States in the mid-1990s.

While considering her future, Lisa played for the gold-medal-winning United States team in the 1994 Goodwill Games in Atlanta, Georgia. In the four games, she couldn't be stopped. Seventy-two percent of her shots from the field hit home (28 out of 39), and she averaged 18 points and 7.3 rebounds. Later that year, she played on the bronze-medal-winning team in the World Championship Games.

For Lisa and other women players, that was as far as they could go in the United States at the time. European nations, however, did have professional leagues for women, and they were on the lookout for good U.S. women players. When a league in Alcamo, Italy, offered Lisa a contract to join the Sicilgesso team, she accepted, playing the 1994–95 season with the squad. As she had done everywhere she played, Lisa became a star, averaging 22.6 points and 11.7 rebounds a game.

Lisa gained a great deal of experience playing in Italy, and although she enjoyed her time there, she did have problems at first. As she recalled, she had difficulty "watching television I didn't really understand," and she struggled with the language. Soon, however, she learned Italian well enough to speak with her teammates and the fans. She also remembered that "Italy was great, especially the food. And the fans are die-hards."

When Lisa left Italy after one season, she was ready to realize a cherished goal—to play in the Olympics.

4

OLYMPIC GLORY

When Lisa returned to the United States, she found that her abilities had not been forgotten. In 1995, when the women's team that would play in the 1996 Olympics held tryouts, coach Tara VanDerveer invited Lisa to attend.

Lisa had entered the Olympic trials once before, in 1990, as the youngest player to try out. She had been a late cut, however. So she was eager to make it this time. Nearly 60 women—the finest basketball players the United States had to offer—were trying out. When the final cuts were decided, the atmosphere was tense as each hopeful was called separately into a room and told her fate by the coach. Lisa survived each cut, and when she got the word she had made the Olympic team, all she could do was shout, "YEAH!"

The training plan for the U.S. team was to play an intense and grueling schedule for more than a year so that individual players could get to know one another and learn to work together as a team. During that period,

---

Lisa outhustles an opponent to complete a pass during the 1996 Olympic Games in Atlanta. Realizing her dream of playing for Team USA in the Olympics, her scoring and rebounds led the U.S. team to a gold medal, while she personally recorded a team best of 29 points.

Lisa and her teammates traveled more than 100,000 miles, playing 52 games on four continents against the best the world had to offer, and they won all 52 games! Lisa's play dominated the games, averaging 17.4 points and seven rebounds per game.

The tour helped shape the players into a team that was determined to win the gold medal in the Olympics. The team also wanted to redeem the reputation of U.S. women's teams that had not fared well in recent international competitions. In the 1992 Olympics, the U.S. women's team had been trounced and had been beaten again in the 1994 World Championship. The players were determined it would not happen another time.

There was added pressure as well. C. M. Newton, the athletic director at the University of Kentucky and the president of USA Basketball, told Coach VanDerveer, "This is not about silver, this is not about bronze. It's about gold." Tara VanDerveer, who had taken a leave from her position as head coach at Stanford University to lead the team, was well aware of the pressures to win. For more than a year, she had worked to mold her players into a cohesive unit, and by the time of the Olympics, she and the U.S. women were ready.

In the first few games in Atlanta, viewers got a taste of what the U.S. team could do. In rapid succession, Lisa and her teammates knocked off Cuba, Ukraine, Zaire, South Korea, Japan, and Australia. Against the surprisingly strong Japanese team, Lisa scored 35 points, a new USA Olympic single-game record. As the importance of the games increased, Lisa became even more of a threat to her opponents.

The Australian team was quite a formidable squad, and the women from Down Under jumped out to a 16-8 lead, at which point Lisa took over. Described as the "unstoppable Lisa Leslie" by the Australian press, she rallied her team to a 15-0 run to turn the game around. Nearly single-handedly she effectively stopped Australia's four great inside players, who combined for only 17 points in the game and were repeatedly kept off the boards by Lisa. The United States overtook their opponents in rebounds 48-25. Lisa finished with 22 points and 13 rebounds in what turned out to be a runaway 93-71 win.

The U.S. win put the squad in the gold-medal game against the Brazilian team, one of the best basketball teams in the world. Brazil had been the victor over the United States in the 1994 World Championship and was the Olympic champion in 1992. Brazil was trying to build a strong basketball tradition to rival that of the United States, and it wanted to win this game as badly as the Americans did.

Brazil's best player was Marta Sobral, who had proven many times over that she too was nearly unstoppable. Sobral was Lisa's responsibility, and coach VanDerveer directed Lisa to play a little farther from the basket than she normally did in order to neutralize Sobral's presence.

At first, the strategy didn't work. Sobral, 6' 2" to Lisa's 6' 5", drove around Lisa at will, and the entire Brazilian team leaped over her to grab rebounds. Lisa was playing perhaps the most important game of her career up to that point, and she was not playing it well.

Coach VanDerveer had no choice but to

take Lisa out of the game. Guard Teresa Evans, who had been the youngest player on the 1984 Olympic team and was the oldest on this team, pulled Lisa to the side. Evans was a veteran of three previous Olympics in which U.S. teams had won one bronze and two gold medals. She told Lisa, "We need you to play the way you've been playing the whole year and take it to 'em. And when you get inside, I want you to finish." Lisa listened attentively and understood what Evans was talking about. "That was my wake-up call," she said later.

Even with the early under-par performance by Lisa and the terrific play by Marta Sobral, the United States led at the half 57-46. In the second half, the U.S. team went on an eight-point run and Sobral was taken out of the game with three fouls. It was all but over then as the United States coasted the rest of the way to win the match 111-87 and take home the gold medal.

It was Lisa who made the difference. Once she got back in the game, she was the Lisa everyone had been cheering for the past year. A terror on offense and defense, she controlled both ends of the court, made an amazing 12 baskets out of 14 attempts, and wound up with 29 points.

In the three medal games, Lisa scored 35, 22, and 29 points respectively and made 38 of her 51 shot attempts from the floor. For the eight Olympic games, she averaged 19.5 points, 7.3 rebounds, 19 assists, and nine steals. Lisa was aware of what the Olympic victory meant for women's basketball. "We accomplished what we set out to do," she said after it was over. "We tried to get women's basketball to the next level. Our game speaks for itself, but

now our names are in the public eye and that's the thing that took the NBA [National Basketball Association] from one level to the next."

The country was indeed becoming very aware of women's basketball. Even as Lisa and her teammates were playing their grueling 52 games on the Olympic training tour and then 8 more in the Olympics themselves, other people were back home forming plans for not one, but two, professional basketball leagues for women in the United States.

Wearing their gold medals, Lisa (second from left) and her teammates raise their arms in celebration of their victory. Knowing how significant their win was for women's basketball, Lisa said, "We accomplished what we set out to do."

5

A PROFESSIONAL
LEAGUE FOR WOMEN

In 1995, it became obvious to basketball promoters that women's games were becoming increasingly popular. Encouraged by the exploits of the apparently unbeatable U.S. national team, promoters saw the potential for a professional women's league. They began laying plans to form a league, to be called the American Basketball League (ABL), which would begin play in the fall of 1996.

The idea of women playing basketball was not new. In the 1890s, shortly after James Naismith, an instructor at a YMCA school in Massachusetts, invented basketball for men, a gymnastics instructor at all-female Smith College introduced the game to her students. Soon, colleges began forming women's teams and playing intercollegiate games.

At first, women's rules were designed to conform to the idea of "ladylike" behavior. Players could not snatch the ball, hold it for more than three seconds, or dribble more than three times. Their outfits too had to reflect proper women's attire—floor-length skirts, long sleeves, and leather shoes. Although burdened with heavy clothing and restrictive rules, women's amateur teams persisted.

Lisa and Val Ackerman show off the jersey of the newly formed WNBA. A former University of Virginia player, Val Ackerman was a moving force behind the formation of a U.S. women's national team, and she was later tapped as the WNBA's first president.

By the 1920s, women's basketball was being recognized around the country. The International Women's Sports Federation was formed, which held its version of the Olympics and included women's basketball. Rules and regulations were changing too, conforming more to those of men's basketball. In 1926, the Amateur Athletic Union sponsored the first national women's championship using men's rules.

Despite its increasing popularity, basketball was still an amateur game for women. Then, in 1936, Orwell Moore formed what is considered the first professional women's basketball team. Called the All-American Red Heads, the team traveled the country, playing men's rules and competing with men's teams. As a promotional gimmick, players had to have red hair—whether natural, dyed, or a wig. They also had to wear makeup, look pretty, and play well.

The All-American Red Heads did play well. With no home base, the team "barnstormed" across North America and played in the Philippines. From 1936 to 1973, the Red Heads racked up a record-breaking number of wins, all against men's teams. In one year alone, 1972, they played 558 games, losing only 84. Orwell's wife, Lorene, a team member for 11 years, alone scored an unheard-of 35,426 points.

For 50 years, the All-American Red Heads thrilled basketball fans with their play and their showmanship. When they retired their jerseys in 1986, however, another women's professional team was still several years in the future. Women's sports were given a boost when, in 1972, Congress passed legislation prohibiting sex discrimination under any educational program, including sports, which received federal funding. This education act, called Title IX,

opened the doors for many young women to participate in all sports, not just basketball.

Despite the contribution of the All-American Red Heads, women's professional basketball was slow to develop and slower to be accepted. In 1978, a professional league was attempted when the Women's Professional Basketball League began playing. Because of poor attendance and financial troubles, the league lasted only three seasons. Over the next several years, a few women tried to play in the NBA or lower-classification professional leagues, but nothing came from their attempts.

The next major effort came in 1991 with the formation of the Liberty Basketball Association (LBA), which used shorter courts and lower baskets. The league lasted for one exhibition game and never played a league schedule. Again, money and attendance were the big problems. The next year, 1992, the Women's World Basketball Association began and ended almost as quickly as the LBA.

Finally, in 1995, the American Basketball League was formed and played its first season in 1996 with eight teams. Unfortunately, the

Women's basketball outfits have come a long way since the 1920s, when these women were obliged to play in the fashion of the times. Shorts and loose-fitting jerseys were acceptable by the 1970s. For today's fast and strenuous games, outfits are designed to give players maximum freedom and mobility.

ABL was very poorly planned and had trouble recruiting players. The league was also plagued with financial problems and could not come up with corporate sponsorship or television contracts. The ABL never became well established.

While the ABL was in its first season, another professional team was approved by the board of governors of the National Basketball Association (NBA)—the Women's National Basketball Association (WNBA), and teams were to be on the courts for the 1997 season. Even though team cities had not yet been announced, the league began to sign players.

On October 18, 1996, less than a week after the ABL began playing, the WNBA announced its first signings, wisely choosing stars from the previous year's Olympic gold-medal-winning team. Rebecca Lobo and Sheryl Swoopes were the first two signed. Lisa Leslie was the third. Over the next few weeks, 13 more players joined.

Then, officials announced the cities and states that would be charter members of the league: Charlotte, Cleveland, Los Angeles, Houston, New York, Phoenix, Sacramento, and Utah. The WNBA choices gave the league an advantage over the ABL, which had placed its franchises in smaller cities. In selecting major cities, the WNBA believed that the population base and already developed fan interest would make it easier to establish the new teams.

The WNBA's next move was to hold its Elite Draft for 16 signed players. These players would form the nucleus for each franchise. Lisa went to the Los Angeles Sparks, her hometown team. Then in April, the league began drafting college players and veteran players who had not yet signed. Soon the eight rosters were filled and practice began.

The WNBA also made a decision about *when* to play that gave the league another advantage over its rival, the ABL. Naismith had invented basketball to be played indoors in the winter, when the weather outside prevented other sports from being played. Basketball remained a winter sport, for both men and women. Thousands of schools, amateur teams, and professional teams began play as soon as the weather turned cold, and the ABL continued the tradition.

The WNBA, however, had a different idea. With all the high school, college, and professional games overwhelming fans in the winter, the WNBA realized there was little room for still more basketball. Taking a bold step, the WNBA announced it would not try to go head-to-head with all the rest of the basketball world. Its initial season was to be played in the summer, when there was little or no competition for the fans' attention. To emphasize its seasonal difference from all other teams, the WNBA announced it would kick off its inaugural season on June 21, the first day of summer.

The WNBA was also clever in giving the league its name. "*Women's* NBA" suggested to fans that it was basketball being played just as it was in the NBA, only by women.

The WNBA began play only a few months after the ABL season ended. Although the ABL played a second season and went into a third, it appeared to be doomed. The teams still could not get enough corporate sponsorship or media coverage. The league was losing money, and the fans were not turning out. The advent of the WNBA served to reduce the fan support even more. About a third of the way through its last season, the ABL called it quits and filed for bankruptcy.

Meanwhile, the WNBA, although not thriving, was holding its own. Each of the eight teams played a 28-game schedule that first year, and the league was divided into an Eastern Conference and a Western Conference. To determine a champion, officials decided on a four-team playoff format. The four teams would be the winners of each conference race, plus the two teams with the next best records, regardless of which conference they were in.

In Lisa's first season with the Los Angeles Sparks, her team finished second in the Western Conference, winning 14 and losing 14. Every team in the Eastern Conference had a better record, however, and the season champions were the Houston Comets, then a team in the Eastern Conference.

Expanding in 1998, the WNBA added teams in Detroit and Washington, D.C., and increased the schedule to 30 games. Houston was moved to the Western Conference, and once again emerged as the champion. Lisa's Sparks again did not make the playoffs, finishing third in their conference with a disappointing record of 12 wins and 18 losses.

In those first two years of WNBA play, Lisa continued to show her prowess. In 1997, she was third in the league in scoring with an average of 15.9 points per game. She led everyone in rebounding by a huge margin—she averaged 9.5 while the runner-up, the Utah Starzz' Wendy Palmer, averaged only 8.0. Lisa was also second in blocked shots, averaging 2.1.

At season's end, Lisa was named to the All-WNBA first team and was one of the finalists for the Women's Pro Basketball ESPY Award, given annually by ESPN. It was a tremendous season for her, but she also wanted a great season for her team as well.

It was not to be, however. In 1998, Lisa's play was brilliant, but she was the Sparks' only bright spot. Once more, she was third in scoring with 19.6; once again, she was the leading rebounder with 10.2; and once again, she was second in blocked shots with 2.1.

Because of her team's poor showing, however, she was a second-team All-WNBA selection, even though she set a new league record for rebounds in a game, ripping down 21 against the Washington Mystics on June 19. She also scored her personal game high of 30 points three times during the season. Although Lisa performed brilliantly, she was not satisfied. The Sparks had not improved over their first year, losing more than they won and dropping a spot in the conference standings.

In each postseason—1997 and 1998—Lisa was with the USA basketball team that played in international competitions. In 1998, the team grabbed the gold medal in the FIBA Women's Basketball World Championship in Germany, winning all nine of its games. Lisa averaged 17.1 points and 8.8 rebounds. For her efforts, she was named USA Basketball's 1998 Female Athlete of the Year, an award she had also won in 1993. Lisa became the fourth player to win the honor more than once.

As the start of the 1999 season drew near, Lisa was ready to play. Unfortunately, however, preseason predictions again did not give the Sparks much of a chance to make the playoffs.

6

AGAINST THE ODDS

In the 1999 season, two new teams were added to the league: the Miracle of Orlando, Florida, joined the Eastern Conference, and the Lynx of Minnesota entered the Western Conference. The schedule was also increased by two games, with each team playing 32 games, and six teams—the top three finishers in each conference—would compete in the playoffs.

The Houston Comets were the favorites to win the Western Conference and take the league title for the third year in a row. No clear-cut second choice emerged, however. There was a little respect for the Sacramento Monarchs, but their support was only lukewarm.

The Sparks' 1999 season got underway on June 20, with Lisa scoring 19 points to lead her team over the Monarchs in the opener for both teams. Two days later, she equaled her professional high-point total with 30, and added 19 rebounds in a 91-59 romp over the defending Eastern Conference champion Cleveland Rockers.

Then the winning streak started to fade, and Lisa's team

An awed crowed watches Lisa in action on the boards. Playing against the odds in the 1999 WNBA playoffs, the Sparks came through with a closing flurry of baskets. Lisa's scoring led her team to a second-place finish and the chance to go on to take the championship.

began to look like the Sparks of 1998. Over the next 10 days, the squad lost a couple, won one, then lost two more. The Sparks dropped to below a winning percentage of 500, which means they had lost more than they won. Even in the game they won during this time, their play was ragged and uneven.

At this point, the Sparks' coach, Orlando Woolridge, had a stern talk with his players. The talk must have had a strong impact on the players as the team kicked it into gear and won the next six games in a row. After a couple of losses, the Sparks won six more in a row. During this second streak, Lisa was at the top of her game. She averaged 19.7 points and 8.7 rebounds in the run to put the team into solid contention for a playoff spot. She was making more than 50 percent of her shots.

Then, as quickly as the Sparks got hot, they cooled off again, and so did Lisa. The team lost five of its next six games, the last four in a row. For Lisa, it was a blow. In those five losses, she averaged fewer than nine points a game and missed nearly two-thirds of her attempted shots. The Sparks had been in second place, but this latest run of poor play dropped them to third, behind both the Comets and the Monarchs.

In the last of those four straight losses, the Sparks fell apart, looking nothing like a playoff contender. They lost to the lowly Washington Mystics, the last-place team in the Eastern Conference, scoring only 53 points, their lowest total in any game all year. Lisa fouled out with only five points. It seemed that her play, and that of her team, had reached a low and could not recover.

The season was not yet over for the Sparks,

however. They bounced back once again and won three of their last four games, enabling them to pass the Monarchs. On August 16, two days after a stunning loss to the Mystics, the Sparks finally downed the Charlotte Sting, the second-place team in the Eastern Conference.

The turnaround was led by Lisa. At half-time, the Sting and the Sparks were tied at 37 points apiece, but another rousing talk by Coach Woolridge spurred his team into action. As the second half began, forward La'Keishia Frett and guard Gordana Grubin repeatedly got the ball to Lisa, whose scoring enabled the Sparks to pull away. By the midpoint of the

Prepping for a game, Lisa stretches her 6′ 5″ frame. Workouts and constant practice keep Lisa in shape on the court as well as off.

Lisa has words of encouragement for a teammate. Although her scoring has led the Sparks to many victories, Lisa is a team player who is quick to acknowledge the other players' support.

half, Lisa and her teammates were ahead by 10 points and they coasted to a 76-65 win. Lisa had played her best game in nearly two weeks, scoring 25 points and making 9 of her 16 shot attempts. Lisa's 25 points were her third-highest single-game point total for the entire season.

The game with the Sting marked a major turning point for the Sparks. Trailing the Monarchs by two games for second place in the Western Conference, the three-win and one-loss finish allowed them to overtake the Monarchs for the second spot.

This closing rush gave the Sparks a record of 20 wins and 12 losses at the season's end. The only team in the entire WNBA with a better record was the Houston Comets, and no team in the Eastern Conference came close.

Lisa didn't accomplish this turnaround alone. She had a fine team playing with her, one that had scored the most points in the league. Because of her supporting cast, Lisa did not try to do everything herself. As a consequence, however, her personal stats were not as impressive as they had been in previous years. Even so, she was eighth in the league in scoring with a 15.6 point average, fourth in rebounds with 7.8 per game, and fourth in blocks rejecting an average of 1.5 in a given game.

Her goal, however, and that of the Sparks, was to win it all. The team had made the playoffs and now they were determined to go all the way to the championship. Getting the trophy meant knocking off two of their Western Conference opponents and then facing the Eastern Conference champ. The road ahead would be rough if Lisa and her team were to go all the way.

The Sparks' first opponent in the playoffs was their tough conference rival, the Sacramento Monarchs. The Monarchs had finished only one game behind the Sparks and had the third-best record in the WNBA. They were also the second-highest scoring team in the league. Both teams seemed to be evenly matched; each had beaten the other twice during the season.

The Sparks were a strong favorite, however. The Monarchs' superstar Yolanda Griffith, second in the league in scoring and blocked shots and first in rebounds, was injured near the season's end. She was out for the playoffs, and the Sparks were given an edge.

As the two teams began the play, however, it was hard to tell which would be the victor. The Monarchs held Lisa and her team to only nine baskets in the first half and held a solid 32-21 lead at halftime. Yolanda Griffith's replacement, Tangela Smith, was the big difference; she led all scorers with 12 points at the break.

Coach Woolridge was not happy with his team's efforts and lectured the players in no uncertain terms. Spurred by the coach's pep talk, Lisa was determined to change the situation in the second half. She and the Sparks outscored their opponents 17-6 in the first few minutes to tie the game at 38 points. At this point, the Sparks were on a roll, outscoring the Monarchs 11-4 in a three-minute period. With 14 minutes left to play, Lisa's team led 49-42 and coasted to a 71-58 win. The Sparks so dominated the game in the second half that Yolanda Griffith admitted in a postgame interview that she didn't think it would have made any difference if she had played.

During that early second-half run, Lisa scored 12 of her 22 points. She also grabbed 12 rebounds in the game. After the game, Lisa stated: "I am very excited. . . . [Coach Woolridge] got on us at halftime, which I think really helped us out. Second half we came out and wanted to play with a lot of heart and I know we did that." Coach Woolridge added, "I am very proud of the effort that the team showed in the second half. The thing about the first half is that I think we were just nervous about being in the playoffs."

The first round of the playoffs was only one

game, with the winner going on to the next round. So the Monarchs went home, and the Sparks had to tackle the mighty Houston Comets in a best two-out-of-three series for the Western Conference championship. In most sports playoffs, when an odd number of teams are involved, the team with the best record does not have to play in the first round. This is called a "bye." Houston had a bye in the first round, and the Comets were well rested and sharp as they waited to confront Lisa and her teammates.

7

GOING FOR
ALL THE MARBLES

The first game of the Western Conference series between the Sparks and the Comets was played in Los Angeles. During the regular season, the two teams had played each other four times, with each team winning its two home-court games.

At the start, the Sparks seemed to be in trouble as the Comets scored the first 8 points. The Sparks finally scored on a layup by Lisa three minutes into the game. For the next eight minutes, the two teams traded buckets.

With about nine minutes left in the first half, Los Angeles went on an 8-2 run to take its first lead with seven minutes remaining. Lisa and teammate Tamecka Dixon scored all 8 points in the spurt. Then, Houston quickly pulled ahead 27-26, but Lisa hit a three-point basket, and the Sparks never trailed again. Their lead was 33-29 at the half, and they came out after halftime with an 11-2 run. A minute later, after trading baskets, Los Angeles scored 9 straight points to build its lead to 44-31.

The Comets were not dead yet, however. They closed the gap to 7 points at 61-54 with five minutes left to play. The

Lisa is rarely out of the spotlight, whether or not her team wins. Hoping for a victory against the Houston Comets in the 1999 WNBA finals, the Sparks were defeated. Lisa's play, however, was outstanding, and as she said, "There's always another year."

Sparks were ready for the challenge and pulled away again to record a final 75-60 victory. Lisa finished with 23 points. This game marked the high point of the Sparks' season. They had gone head-to-head with the mighty, two-time championship Comets in the most important game of the year to that point and beat them convincingly.

The next two games, however, were in Houston, where the Comets had won 15 out of 16 games in 1999 and the last 12 in a row. In 6 games over the three years of the WNBA's existence, Los Angeles had *never* won in the Comets' hometown.

In the first playoff game in Houston, Lisa and the Sparks were a disaster. Although down by only six points at halftime, they never got any closer in the second half. Frustrated by the team's poor play, Los Angeles guard DeLisha Milton committed a flagrant foul, tripping Tammy Jackson of the Comets with 11 minutes left in the game. She was immediately ejected. When Coach Woolridge argued with the referee over the decision he, too, was thrown out. Houston was awarded three free throws, one for the tripping foul and two for the technical foul. The Comets made all three and then ran the score up to the final 83-55.

Lisa failed to hit a field goal until the middle of the second half, when she hit a three-pointer. She made only four buckets out of her 13 attempts and ended up with only 11 points. But she did take eight rebounds and dish out four assists. Overall, though, no one on the team played well.

It came down to game three for the Western Conference title. The Sparks had won the first game fairly easily, and the Comets had run away

Lisa reaches out with her long limbs to grab the ball from Comet Tina Thompson. Although rivals in the WNBA championship finals, the two played together on the 1999 All-WNBA second team.

with game two. Until this point, Los Angeles had been shut out in Houston in seven tries, and the Comets had won 13 games in a row on their home court. The Sparks' fans were hoping that number 13 would be unlucky for the Comets.

The deciding game was played hard by both teams. In the first half, neither team could get the upper hand. In the second half, the Sparks got a four-point lead and were holding at 53-49. Then the Comets' Cynthia Cooper hit a three-pointer, and Lisa came back with a layup.

Fighting back, Houston scored seven in a row to take a 59-55 lead. The Sparks wouldn't quit. Twice they closed the gap to two points, and with five minutes remaining, Lisa's basket made it 61-59. The Comets' defense played tough and prevented the Sparks from scoring over the next three minutes, while they pulled ahead.

With only one minute to go and the game safely in Houston's hands, Comet Tina Thompson, who had been a teammate of Lisa's in school, began taunting the Sparks star. Frustrated by the impending defeat, Lisa countered by shoving Thompson, and both players were ejected. Still, Lisa had played an outstanding game, scoring 20 points and pulling down seven rebounds in the 72-62 loss. The Sparks' season was over.

Even in defeat, Lisa was upbeat. She commented after the game, "I think this Comets team knows that they just went through the best team in the WNBA and I wish them the best of luck. I'm sure they won't have as hard a time with New York."

Even though her team had lost the finals of the Western Conference, Lisa's overall play had been impressive. For the four playoff games—one against Sacramento and three against Houston—she averaged 19 points and 8.5 rebounds. Lisa was looking forward to a rematch. "We're still moving ahead, there's always another year," she said.

Lisa's prediction about Houston and New York was right on target. The Comets defeated the Eastern Conference playoff winner, the New York Liberty, in three games to win their third straight WNBA title. In game two, Teresa Weatherspoon of the Liberty threw a nearly impossible shot from 50 feet at the final buzzer.

This incredible shot led New York to a 68-67 win and kept the Comets from sweeping the series in two games.

Although Lisa's personal season statistics were down as a result of her teammates' excellent play, she no longer had to carry the full load on her shoulders. She knew that others could also score and rebound. Because of the decline in those personal numbers, however, she had to settle for being named to the All-WNBA second team.

Nevertheless, 1999 was an exciting year for Lisa and the Sparks. She is determined to stay ahead of the competition and keep the team there with her. Even with all her success, Lisa doesn't let up. She describes her daily routine after the season: "I do weights in the morning, I play basketball with a private trainer and some NBA players. Then I play pick-up in the evenings from 4 to 6."

When Lisa was asked what is the best part of being a professional athlete, she replied, "During the season, the best part about it is getting to be a role model for younger girls and being around your teammates all the time."

The 1999 season was also a year of distinction for the WNBA. For the first time in the league's three-year history, the average attendance for the regular-season games exceeded 10,000 people.

Lisa has basketball plans for the winter of 1999–2000. Once again, she will tour with the USA basketball team and she will play in the first WNBA Hall of Fame game with and against other WNBA stars.

8

IN THE REAL WORLD

L isa Leslie's life is far more than playing basketball. Although she devotes a great deal of time to her game during the year, she continues with her many other activities and business pursuits and is deeply involved in the activities of the community.

In 1996, before the WNBA began play, she signed a contract with the famous Wilhelmina Models, Inc. and continues to model when she has time. She also intends to continue modeling after her basketball days are over. Her modeling jobs so far have included a photo spread of Olympic athletes for *Vogue* magazine and a feature in a *Newsweek* magazine ad. Lisa has also been on the runway to show off both Armani and Tommy Hilfiger fashions.

Does she have a favorite aspect of modeling? "All the levels of modeling are so different that I don't think I can pick a favorite," she replied. "I love all types of modeling, whether it be on a runway in front of hundreds of people, or the photo shoot where it's just me and the photographer. It gives me a chance to let people know that there's much more to Lisa Leslie. I also like to show girls that you can be

---

In the world off the court, Lisa devotes as much time as she can to working in the community. She is especially interested in encouraging young women to get into sports, as she is doing here, teaching at a basketball clinic in Los Angeles.

tough and feminine, too."

Lisa's youthful interest in becoming a weather reporter has changed to being a sportscaster. She frequently does the color commentary for the basketball games of her alma mater, USC, and she does some correspondence reporting on *NBA Inside Stuff*. She also plans to pursue acting in the future and has already been a guest star on several TV shows, including *Moesha* and *Hang Time*. In the future, "I'd love to play a superhero," she says.

Lisa is also involved as a Nike endorser and has contracts with Sears, Pepsi, and General Motors. Such endorsements pay handsomely, but they also take much of her time, which she tries to divide among all her pursuits. Lisa also owns her own company, Lisa Leslie Enterprises, of which she is the chief executive officer. With all that she is involved in, is there a problem in handling her off-court undertakings and her basketball career? Not at all, she answers. "As far as balancing my careers, it's all about focus. I think focus is what has enabled me to excel in life. When I play basketball, there is absolutely nothing else on my mind. When I'm modeling, I'm focused on modeling and doing the best I can for the photographer or audience. When I'm a special correspondent for *NBA Inside Stuff*, I'm totally focused on what I need to do to give the best interview possible."

These are personal activities and goals, however. Much more important is her community-related work. She talks about her involvement: "I'm a board member of my church and I give a lot of donations to them. I do a program called 'Taking it Inside with Lisa Leslie' and another one, OGDL, which is the Olympic Girls Development League, which is also the league that

I grew up playing in. The Taking it Inside program does just that; we go into classrooms and give them all booklets called 'The World Is My Playground.' The booklets focus on goals and self-esteem for young girls and teaching them to have a positive outlook on life."

Lisa is also deeply committed to working with foster children, and because of them, she became certified in cardiopulmonary resuscitation (CPR). As she has explained: "My boyfriend and I met [foster kids] through church and we loved spending time with them. At first we'd only see them every once in a while, but now

Lisa endorses products and does modeling just as other sports superstars do. Here she is on the set of a shoot for a Nike shoe commercial. Leaning on crutches and watching (at left) is the well-known movie director Spike Lee.

"Talk about a slam dunk," proclaims this ad featuring Lisa and players Sheryl Swoopes (left) and Nikki McCray (right). Although rivals on the court—Sheryl is a Comet and Nikki plays with the Washington Mystics—the three athletes got together to promote drinking milk for one of the famous "milk mustache" ads.

we see them every Sunday and have dinner with them at least twice a month. I had a photo shoot in L. A. with Scottie Pippen and they got to come along, so I think that was a lot of fun for them."

Visibly moved, Lisa continued, "We became really close with them and their guardian told us that they could stay with us at my house if we got certified [in CPR/life saving]. So we started taking the classes and I really liked it. I'm proud of it now because I could save somebody's life if I was ever in that situation."

Lisa is also a spokesperson for Big Brothers Big Sisters of America, a charity in which she strongly believes. "I chose this charity in particular because I think it's very important that kids have role models to look up to. My mom made sure that I was raised properly and was given all the support I needed. Big Brothers Big Sisters of America is focused on providing youth with the necessary support when they can't receive it at home."

To continue her interest in helping children, Lisa also participated in a Self-Esteem Symposium, Helping Girls Become Strong Women. Workshops presented practical skills for teens including building healthy self-esteem, setting goals, and overcoming stress. The workshops also dealt with body image, which is particularly important to Lisa because she was so tall and was teased about her height at a young age.

Lisa remembers her roots. Thanks to her, Morningside High School has the Lisa Leslie Sports Complex. So far, it consists of a 42,000 square-foot basketball court with 12 baskets, donated by Nike on behalf of Lisa. Eventually the complex will include facilities for track, baseball, soccer, and tennis.

Roosevelt Dorn, mayor of Lisa's hometown of Inglewood, was present at the dedication of the complex. "It's a great thing when you've made it in life and not forgotten where you came from," he said in praise of Lisa. "That's what it's about. Lisa has come back and is giving back."

Clearly moved by the ceremony, Lisa shed tears as she spoke. "I'm so thankful that I have the opportunity to share with you what I've done. I want you to know that I sat where you sit right now," she said amidst thundering applause from the hundreds of students, teachers, and guests gathered for the event.

This is the life of Lisa Leslie off the court,

but on the court is where she intends to stay for as long as she can. She has advice for young players who want to play basketball at higher levels. "The first thing I would say is put God first," she began. "The second thing is that you're going to get out of it what you put into it. You have to practice a lot. I used to spend hours a day in the gym, taking about 500 shots each day from all over the court. I also recommend to girls to always try to practice with boys because it will make you a better player."

That regimen certainly has worked for Lisa. Determination, practice, and being the best that you can be has made it possible for her to reach her goals in life. "I always wanted to play pro basketball . . . not in Europe, not in Japan . . . but pro basketball in the USA. That was my dream as a kid and now that the WNBA will be providing me that opportunity, it's a dream come true."

STATISTICS

COLLEGE

Year	Team	G	FGM	FGA	Pct.	FTM	FTA	Pct.	REB	AST	PTS	AVG
1990–91	USC	30	241	504	.478	98	145	.676	299	20	582	19.4
1991–92	USC	31	262	476	.550	104	152	.697	261	46	632	20.4
1992–93	USC	29	211	378	.558	119	162	.735	285	58	543	18.7
1993–94	USC	30	259	464	.558	138	201	.687	369	83	657	21.9
TOTALS		120	973	1822	.536	459	660	.695	1214	207	2414	20.1

WNBA

Year	Team	G	FGM	FGA	Pct.	FTM	FTA	Pct.	REB	AST	PTS	AVG
1997	Los Angeles	28	160	371	.431	113	189	.598	266	74	445	15.9
1998	Los Angeles	28	202	423	.478	136	171	.768	285	70	549	19.6
1999	Los Angeles	32	182	389	.468	114	156	.731	248	54	500	15.6
TOTALS		88	544	1183	.459	363	516	.703	799	198	1494	17.0

WNBA Playoffs

Year	Team	G	FGM	FGA	Pct.	FTM	FTA	Pct.	REB	AST	PTS	AVG
1999	Los Angeles	4	29	60	.483	14	18	.778	34	11	76	19.0

G	Games Played	FTA	Free Throws Attempted
FGM	Field Goals Made	REB	Rebounds
FGA	Field Goals Attempted	AST	Assists
Pct.	Percentage	PTS	Points
FTM	Free Throws Made	AVG	Average

CHRONOLOGY

1972	Born in Inglewood, California, on July 7
1976	Father leaves the family; mother becomes a truck driver
1984	Tries out for the junior high school basketball team
1990	Scores 101 points in the first half of a high school game; named Naismith Prep Player of the Year; enters USC
1991–94	Earns All-America honors each season
1994	Named Naismith College Player of the Year
1994–95	Plays professional basketball in Italy
1996	Leads United States Olympic team to the gold medal
1997	Plays for the Los Angeles Sparks in the first season of the WNBA; named first team All-WNBA
1999	Selected as MVP of the first WNBA All-Star game; leads the Sparks into the playoffs for the first time

FURTHER READING

Gogol, Sara. *Playing in a New League: The Women of the American Basketball League's First Season.* Mamaroneck, NY: Masters Press, 1998.

Gutman, Bill. *Shooting Stars: The Women of Pro Basketball.* New York: Random House, 1998.

Ponti, James. *WNBA: Stars of Women's Basketball.* New York: Archway, 1999.

VanDerveer, Tara. *Shooting from the Outside: How a Coach and Her Olympic Team Transformed Women's Basketball.* New York: Avon, 1998.

Whiteside, Kelly. *WNBA: A Celebration: Commemorating the Birth of a League.* New York: HarperCollins, 1998.

ABOUT THE AUTHOR

BRENT KELLEY is an equine veterinarian and a writer. He is the author of 10 books on baseball history and two (using the pen name Grant Kendall) on his experiences as a veterinarian, as well as the title *Keith Van Horn* in Chelsea House's BASKETBALL LEGENDS series. He is a columnist for *Thoroughbred Times*, a weekly horse racing and breeding publication, and *Bourbon Times*, a weekly family newspaper. He has written more than 400 articles for various magazines and newspapers. He lives in Paris, Kentucky, with his wife, children, and animals.

HANNAH STORM, NBC Sports play-by-play announcer, reporter, and studio host, made her debut in 1992 at Wimbledon during the All England Tennis Championships. Shortly thereafter, she was paired with Jim Lampley to cohost the *Olympic Show* for the 1992 Olympic Games in Barcelona. Later that year, Storm was named cohost of *Notre Dame Saturday*, NBC's college football pregame show. Adding to her repertoire, Storm became a reporter for the 1994 Major League All-Star Game and the pregame host for the 1995, 1997, and 1999 World Series. Storm's success as host of *NBA Showtime* during the 1997-98 season won her the role as studio host for the inaugural season of the Women's National Basketball Association in 1998.

In 1996, Storm was selected as NBC's host for the Summer Olympics in Atlanta, and she has been named as host for both the 2000 Summer Olympics in Sydney and the 2002 Winter Olympics in Salt Lake City. Storm received a Gracie Allen Award for Outstanding Personal Achievement, which was presented by the American Women in Radio and Television Foundation (AWRTF), for her coverage of the 1999 NBA Finals and 1999 World Series. She has been married to NBC Sports broadcaster Dan Hicks since 1994. They have two daughters.

INDEX

All-American honors, 9, 19, 22, 23

All-American Red Heads, 34, 35

All-PAC-10, 22, 23

All-State honors, 19

All-WNBA team, 9, 38, 39

Amateur Athletic Union, 34

American Basketball League, 10, 33, 35-36, 36

Chancellor, Van, 12

Charlotte Sting, 43-44

Dorn, Roosevelt, 59

Eastern Conference, 10, 12, 38, 41, 42, 43, 45

Evans, Teresa, 30

Female Athlete of the Year, 39

FIBA Women's Basketball World Championship, 39

Gatorade Player of the Year, 19

Goodwill Games, 24-25

Hargrove, Sharon, 16

Houston Comets, 10, 12, 38, 41, 42, 45, 47, 49-53

International Women's Sports Federation, 34

Italy, 25

Jones Cup, 23

Junior World Championship team, 17

Kodak All-American Award, 23

Lady Trojans, 21-24

Leslie, Christine (mother), 15-16

Leslie, Dionne (sister), 15, 16

Leslie, Lisa
  birth of, 15
  business pursuits of, 55-56
  childhood of, 15-17
  community work of, 56-59
  education of, 16, 17-18, 21-24
  and endorsements, 56
  family of, 15-16

Leslie, Tiffany (sister), 15, 16

Liberty Basketball Association, 35

Los Angeles Sparks, 9, 36, 38, 39, 41-47, 49-53

Moore, Orwell, 34

Morningside High School, 17-19, 59

Most Valuable Player (MVP), 9-13

Naismith, James, 19, 33, 37

Naismith College Player of the Year, 9, 23

Naismith Prep Player of the Year, 19

National Collegiate Athletic Association Tournament, 22, 23

National Freshman of the Year, 9, 22

National Player of the Year, 9, 23

Newton, C. M., 28

New York Liberty, 52-53

Olympics, 25, 27-31

PAC-10 Freshman of the Year, 22

PAC-10 Player of the Week, 22

Sacramento Monarchs, 41, 42, 44-47

Scott, Frank, 17, 18, 19

Title IX, 34-35

University of Southern California, 21-24, 56

USA Basketball, 28, 39, 53

USA Basketball Player of the Year, 23

USA Today Prep Player of the Year, 19

VanDerveer, Tara, 27, 28, 29-30

Washington Mystics, 39, 42, 43

Western Conference, 10, 12, 38, 41, 44, 45, 47, 49-53

WNBA All-Star game, 9-13

WNBA Hall of Fame game, 53

Women's National Basketball Association, 9-10, 36-38, 41, 53, 60

Women's Pro Basketball ESPY Award, 38

Women's Professional Basketball League, 35

Women's World Basketball Association, 35

Woolridge, Orlando, 42, 43, 46, 50

World Championships, 23, 25, 28, 29

World University Games, 22